Transforming Displays

Comprehending OLED and Mini-LED

Taylor Royce

DEDICATION

This book is dedicated to all the innovators who dared to dream bigger than what was possible and to the innumerable people whose curiosity and passion propel the rapidly changing field of technology.

May this effort serve as a tribute to your unwavering pursuit of greatness and a proof of the transformational potential of creativity and vision. Your efforts have inspired and shaped the future, and for that, I am incredibly appreciative.

To my loved ones, whose steadfast encouragement and support have been the cornerstone of my path. This is made possible by your confidence in my efforts.

And to the readers, I hope these pages provide you with inspiration to explore, develop, and push the boundaries of what is possible in addition to providing insights into the future of display technology.

CONTENTS

ACKNOWLEDGMENTS

My sincere appreciation goes out to everyone who helped and advised me while I was writing this book.

I want to start by sincerely thanking the professionals and experts in the field of display technology. Your knowledge, experience, and research have greatly influenced the content of this book. Your contributions have given us a strong basis on which to comprehend the advancements and difficulties of display technologies.

I would especially like to express my gratitude to my family and friends for their continuous support and inspiration. Your patience and faith in my vision have been crucial to finishing this project. Thanks to your understanding and sacrifices, this trip has been both incredibly rewarding and achievable.

I am also appreciative of my mentors and coworkers who gave of their time and expertise to evaluate drafts and offer helpful criticism. This work has been much improved by your advice, and your knowledge has served as an inspiration.

Thank you to the editorial team and publishers for your hard work and professionalism in making this book a reality. Throughout the publication process, we have tremendously appreciated your dedication to excellence.

Lastly, I would like to thank all of my readers for their interest in this work. The quest of knowledge and innovation is motivated by your inquisitiveness and desire to comprehend the direction that display technology is taking. It is my goal that this study gives you useful insights and encourages more research in this exciting area.

I appreciate all of your help and inspiration. This book is the result of both my own work and your inputs.

DISCLAIMER

This book's content is just meant to serve as general information, and it was written using the most recent research and industry standards accessible. Although every effort has been taken to assure the content's authenticity and dependability, new advances in the field of display technology may have emerged following this book's publication.

Regarding the material provided herein, its accuracy, completeness, or fitness for any particular purpose, the author and publisher make no claims or warranties. Before making judgments based on the material in this book, the reader should confirm any facts and, if needed, consult a specialist.

Both the publisher and the author disclaim all liability for any mistakes or omissions that may occur when using the information in this book. The author's opinions and views do not necessarily represent those of any organizations or people that are referenced.

CHAPTER 1

1.1 A Look Back at Display Technologies: From Cathode Ray Tubes to Contemporary Flat Panels

The development of display technologies has been an exciting path filled with important breakthroughs and rapid advancements in technology. Cathode Ray Tubes (CRTs) were the first step on this path, and today's flat-panel displays are the most popular on the market. Gaining an understanding of this historical trajectory might help you better understand the developments that have influenced the state of display technology today.

- **CRTs (cathode ray tubes):** The first commonly used display technology was CRTs, which introduced in the early 20th century. They worked by aiming an electron beam at a phosphorescent screen, which produced light in the shape of images.

Although CRTs were large, heavy, and power-hungry, they provided dependable performance for many years. Deep blacks and brilliant colors were produced by CRTs, in spite of their small size—achievements that many contemporary technologies still try to match.

- **The Shift to Level Panels:** The size and energy usage constraints of CRTs prompted the creation of flat-panel displays. When liquid crystal displays (LCDs) were first introduced in the 1980s, this change got underway. LCDs were more suited for a variety of applications, including televisions and computer displays, because they were lighter and considerably thinner than CRTs. LCDs were made possible by liquid crystals, which could control light flow to create images when positioned in certain ways.

- **Plastic-Panel Display Developments:** The technology behind flat panels has developed more over time. Despite their brief lifespan, plasma screens had superior contrast ratios and color reproduction over early LCD models. But gradually, advances in LCD technology—especially with the advent of LED backlighting—surpassed them. Even thinner screens with higher brightness and energy efficiency are now possible thanks to LED (Light Emitting Diode) technology.

- **The Rise of OLED and Beyond:** The development of Organic Light Emitting Diode (OLED) technology resulted in a notable improvement in display quality. OLED displays, in contrast to LCDs, don't need a backlight because each pixel emits light on its own. Deeper blacks, greater contrast ratios, and more vivid colors are made possible as a result. OLED technology is now standard in expensive smartphones, TVs, and monitors. Furthermore, cutting-edge technologies like Micro-LED and Mini-LED are expanding the possibilities by providing previously unheard-of levels of brightness and color fidelity.

1.2 Basic Display Technology Principles: Color Reproduction, Backlighting, and Pixel Structure

In order to have a complete understanding of contemporary display technologies, one must grasp the basic ideas that underpin their functionality. Pixel structure, backlighting, and color reproduction are some of these elements that are crucial in establishing the quality of images we see on screens.

- **Pixel Organization:** The pixel, the smallest unit of a digital image, is at the center of every display. The three fundamental colors red, green, and blue (RGB) are displayed by the sub-pixels that make up each pixel. Through adjustment of these sub-pixels' intensity, a display can generate an extensive spectrum of colors. The resolution—also called pixel density and arrangement—determines the image's clarity and sharpness. Images with higher resolutions—like 4K and 8K—have more pixels per inch, making them sharper and more detailed.

- **Backlighting:** The majority of contemporary

displays, especially LCDs, depend on backlighting to illuminate the pixels. The overall quality of the display can be greatly impacted by the sort of illumination that is employed. The backlighting of traditional LCDs was provided by Cold Cathode Fluorescent Lamps (CCFL), but LED backlighting which uses less energy and enables thinner panels has essentially superseded this. It is possible to have edge-lit or full-array LED backlighting. Edge-lit screens are slimmer, but full-array displays, with their ability to independently dim or brighten different zones of the panel, provide superior control over brightness and contrast.

- **Reproduction of Color:** One important aspect of a display's quality is how well it can replicate colors. The backlighting system and the pixel structure work together in this. For example, the ability of individual pixels to be turned on or off allows OLED displays to reproduce color with exceptional accuracy, resulting in genuine blacks and a wide color range. However, because their backlights are unable to produce the same contrast, classic LCDs frequently display colors with poorer accuracy. By enabling displays to accommodate a wider variety of brightness levels, color management innovations like High Dynamic variety (HDR) significantly improve color accuracy and produce more lifelike images.

1.3 Overview of OLED and Mini-LED: Fundamental Ideas and Features

Mini-LED and OLED have emerged as two of the most promising advancements in display technology. Both technologies have unique benefits, and recognizing their influence on the market requires a comprehension of their fundamental ideas and workings.

- **Mini-LED Innovation:** The advancement of conventional LED backlighting, known as mini-LED, uses much smaller LEDs that may be arranged into a greater number of dimming zones. The halo effect sometimes observed in conventional LED displays is lessened by the greater granularity, which enables more exact control over brightness and contrast. Mini-LED technology is especially useful for HDR video since it can display dazzling highlights and deep blacks, which is an essential feature. It is perfect for usage in bright conditions since it offers higher peak brightness levels than OLED.

- **OLED Technology:** In contrast, OLED technology functions based on a fundamentally distinct concept. OLED does not require a backlight, in contrast to Mini-LED. Rather, organic compounds that generate light when an electric current flows through them make up each pixel. Because self-emissive pixels may be fully turned off, OLED displays can achieve perfect blacks and an infinite contrast ratio. OLED displays are also superior to most other technologies in that they have faster response times and wider viewing angles, which makes them perfect for virtual reality gadgets, smartphones, and high-end televisions.

- **Comparison of OLED and Mini-LED:** Although Mini-LED and OLED provide notable enhancements over conventional LCDs, they possess distinct advantages and disadvantages. Higher brightness levels and a decreased risk of burn-in—a condition where static images cause permanent markings on the screen—are two characteristics of mini-LED displays. OLED screens, on the other hand, provide excellent viewing angles, contrast, and color accuracy. User preferences and the particular application are generally the deciding factors when choosing between the two. For a home theater system, for example, if performance in a dark room is important, OLED might be favored, although Mini-LED might work better under bright, ambient lighting.

1.4 The Search for Visual Perfection: The Significance of Display Quality in the Consumption of Modern Media

Display quality has become a crucial consideration while consuming media in the digital age. There has never been a greater need for high-quality displays, whether for working on creative projects, playing video games, or viewing movies. The significance of display quality and the different elements that go into achieving visual perfection are discussed in this section.

- **Effect on Amusement:** Superior screens improve the watching experience by offering more realistic and immersive images. A display with wide viewing angles, high contrast ratios, and accurate color reproduction, for example, guarantees that the content is viewed as intended by the producers when watching a movie. Premium displays now come equipped with features like broad color gamut support, HDR, and 4K resolution, which provide viewers a movie theater-like experience at home.

- **Performance in Gaming:** Playability is directly impacted by display quality for gamers. In fast-paced games like first-person shooters, a display with a high refresh rate (such 120Hz or 240Hz) and low response time is necessary for fluid and responsive gameplay. Additionally, to lessen screen tearing and make sure the display keeps up with the fast-paced action of the game, features like Variable Refresh Rate (VRR) and low input lag are essential.

Gamers frequently choose OLED displays because of their quick response times and deep blacks, but Mini-LED panels are also becoming more and more well-liked because of their excellent HDR performance and high brightness.

- **Workplace Utilization:** Display quality is not merely a luxury; for professionals in industries like graphic design, photography, and video editing, it is an absolute must. To guarantee that the content they generate will seem consistent across all platforms and media, accurate color reproduction is essential. More detailed work is possible with high-resolution monitors, especially when editing photos or videos. To achieve the best possible color accuracy, professionals frequently utilize calibrated monitors that follow industry standards, such as Adobe RGB or DCI-P3 color schemes.

- **Next Developments:** The quest for visual perfection will probably spur additional advancements in display technology as technology develops. Innovations like Micro-LED, which combines the greatest features of OLED and Mini-LED, has the potential to provide even better performance. Furthermore, developments in machine learning and artificial intelligence may allow displays to adjust to the information being viewed, improving visual quality instantly. The continuous efforts to lower power consumption and enhance durability will also have a big impact on how display technologies develop in the future.

The development of display technologies across time from the first CRTs to the most recent developments in OLED and Mini-LED reflects the ongoing quest for ideal visuals. Anyone interested in media consumption, gaming, or professional creative work will need to grasp the core ideas and advances driving this industry as display technology develops. It is impossible to exaggerate how crucial display quality is because it has a direct effect on how we interact with digital material and how we watch it all together.

CHAPTER 2

IN-DEPTH EXPLORATION OF MINI-LED TECHNOLOGY

2.1 Mini-LED Display Architecture: Configuring LED Arrays, Local Dimming Zones, and Light Control

Thanks to its creative architecture, mini-LED technology constitutes a major breakthrough in display technology. To fully appreciate how Mini-LED displays achieve greater performance in terms of contrast, brightness, and color accuracy, it is imperative to understand their fundamental structure.

- **Zones for Local Dimming:** The utilization of local dimming zones is one of Mini-LED technology's most distinctive features. Mini-LED displays separate the backlight into hundreds or even thousands of independently controlled zones, in contrast to typical LED displays that illuminate the entire backlight uniformly. Numerous tiny LEDs make up each zone, which can be adjusted in brightness or dimness to suit the content being displayed. The display's overall contrast is improved by the fine control over specific zones, which enables significantly deeper blacks and brighter highlights.

- **LED Array Setting:** Another crucial component of Mini-LED architecture is the arrangement of the LED array. Because mini-LEDs are so much smaller than regular LEDs, more lights can be arranged densely behind the screen. More precise light control and intricate local dimming are made possible by this dense array of LEDs. The display can more faithfully simulate minute variations in brightness the more LEDs there are in the array, producing visuals that are more lifelike and engaging.

- **Control Systems for Lighting:** Mini-LED displays use a combination of hardware and software to regulate the light. The software component consists of algorithms that control the brightness and dimming of each zone in accordance with the content of the images, whilst the hardware component consists of the exact placement and functioning of the LED array. Innovative light control systems lessen undesirable effects such as blooming, which occurs when light from bright regions spills into darker regions. This makes Mini-LED displays especially useful for high dynamic range (HDR) material, which necessitates a wide range of luminance.

2.2 Technical Aspects of Mini-LED: Manufacturing of Mini LED Chips, Quantum Dot Integration, and Backlight Design

Numerous significant advancements in manufacturing techniques, backlight design, and quantum dot integration have contributed to the technical sophistication of Mini-LED displays. Each of these elements plays a part in the overall effectiveness and performance of Mini-LED displays.

- **Design of the Backlight:** Compared to traditional LED displays, mini-LED displays have a more sophisticated lighting system. Because Mini-LEDs are smaller than regular LEDs, more LEDs can be positioned in the same space, producing a more even and effective backlight. Screen uniformity difficulties, in which different areas of the screen may seem brighter or darker, are lessened by this design. Mini-LED backlights are also perfect for HDR content and high ambient light settings since they can reach higher peak brightness levels without noticeably affecting power consumption.

- **Integration of Quantum Dots:** Quantum dots are integrated into several Mini-LED displays to improve color performance. When exposed to light, quantum dots tiny semiconductor particles emit light with particular wavelengths. Mini-LED displays can offer a larger color range and more accurate color reproduction by adding quantum dots to the backlight system. This is especially helpful for applications where color fidelity is crucial, such high-end televisions and professional video editing. Because quantum dot integration enables more accurate control over color output, it also contributes to the display's increased energy efficiency.

- **Mini LED Chip Production:** Mini-LED chip manufacture is a difficult process that calls for both sophisticated materials and precise engineering. Care must be taken during the downsizing process of LEDs to guarantee the durability and efficiency of the chips. Growing the LED components on a substrate, then cutting and assembling them into arrays, is the usual procedure. Thinner and more flexible Mini-LED panels are now possible thanks to recent developments in chip manufacturing, which is essential for producing displays that are lightweight and high-performing.

2.3 Mini-LED Display Benefits: Enhanced Color Accuracy, Brightness, and Contrast

Compared to conventional LED and even certain OLED displays, mini-LED displays have a number of advantages, especially when it comes to contrast, brightness, and color accuracy. Mini-LED technology is an appealing option for a variety of applications because of these qualities.

- **Increased Contrast:** Mini-LED displays provide noticeably higher contrast because they can regulate thousands of local dimming zones. This technology produces bright whites and deep blacks, which make for a more dynamic and engaging viewing experience. This is particularly evident with HDR content, where there can be a significant contrast between an image's brightest and darkest areas. By precisely controlling each dimming zone, halo effects are reduced and image quality is further enhanced.

- **Enhanced Vibrance:** Displays can achieve greater maximum brightness levels than conventional LED displays thanks to mini-LED technology. Because of this, they're perfect for using in bright spaces or watching HDR content, which needs a high brightness to properly show off the detail. Mini-LED displays with high brightness levels are ideal for portable electronics like tablets and laptops because they enhance visibility in outdoor environments. Furthermore, because Mini-LED technology uses sophisticated backlighting techniques, the increased brightness is achieved without sacrificing energy economy.

- **Enhanced Color Precision:** Mini-LED displays provide excellent color accuracy because of the incorporation of quantum dots and sophisticated light management technologies. Their ability to accurately reproduce colors and span a larger color range is crucial for jobs like picture and video editing that call for precise color representation. Mini-LED displays have an edge over many other display technologies since they can display a wide range of colors without distortion or oversaturation.

2.4 Mini-LED Technology's Drawbacks and Challenges: Cost, Power Consumption, and Blooming

Although Mini-LED technology has many benefits, it also has some drawbacks and difficulties. These include problems with blooming, cost, and power consumption that must be taken into account when assessing Mini-LED displays' overall efficacy.

- **In bloom:** Blooming is still a possible problem even with Mini-LED displays' sophisticated light control. A halo effect is produced when light from bright regions of the screen leaks into darker ones, a phenomenon known as blooming. Scenes with strong contrast, like white writing on a dark background, make this very obvious. Even though mini-LED displays manage blooming better than conventional LED displays, it is still a possibility. The number of local dimming zones and the efficiency of the algorithms employed to manage them determine how much blooming occurs.

- **High Price**: Higher production costs are a result of the complexity of Mini-LED technology, especially with regard to its backlight design and manufacturing procedures. This ultimately results in increased costs for customers. Mini-LED displays are currently a premium alternative, but as the technology advances and production grows up, pricing should come down. In more cost-conscious areas, the adoption of Mini-LED technology may be constrained, at least initially.

- **Power Requirement:** Mini-LED displays can nevertheless use more power than OLED displays, even though they are typically more energy-efficient than conventional LED displays—especially when they are operating at maximum brightness. Energy usage may rise as a result of the dense array of Mini-LEDs needing more power to produce the appropriate brightness and contrast levels. For battery-operated devices like laptops and tablets, where power economy is crucial, this is an important factor to take into account. Although manufacturers are always trying to increase Mini-LED display power efficiency, there is still a problem that has to be solved.

Mini-LED technology offers improved contrast, brightness, and color accuracy, and it marks a major advancement in display innovation. It does not, however, come without difficulties, such as problems with cost, power consumption, and blooming. These difficulties will probably be lessened as technology develops, increasing

Mini-LED displays' competitiveness in the market. As of right now, Mini-LEDs continue to be a strong choice for anyone looking for high-quality display performance, especially in situations where brightness and contrast are crucial.

CHAPTER 3

OLED TECHNOLOGY EXPLORATION

3.1 The Principle of Organic Light Emitting Diodes (OLEDs): Self-Brightening Pixels and Pixel-Level Management

As opposed to conventional LED and LCD displays, OLED (Organic Light Emitting Diode) technology is based on its self-illuminating pixels and precise pixel-level control.

- **Intelligent Pixels:** In contrast to traditional LED-backlit displays, which use a separate backlight to illuminate the panel, an OLED display's pixels individually emit light. Organic substances that release light in response to an electric current are what enable this. The two electrodes that these organic materials are positioned between are usually transparent ones. The material emits light when electricity flows through it, and this is what we see on the screen. OLEDs are able to provide true blacks because of their self-illumination feature, which enables pixels to be fully shut off and output no light in certain places.

- **Control at the Pixel Level:** OLED technology provides unmatched control at the pixel level. The brightness and hue of each pixel can be separately changed, giving the display's visual output exact control. High contrast ratios and detailed image rendering are dependent on this pixel-level management, particularly in situations with a mix of bright and dark parts. As demonstrated by Mini-LED technology, the ability to operate each pixel independently also lessens the requirement for intricate backlight arrangements, resulting in thinner and lighter display designs.

3.2 Fabrication and Structure of OLED Displays: Material Science and Production Procedures

Advanced material science and precise manufacturing

techniques are fundamental to the structure and manufacture of OLED displays, contributing to their unique features and functionality.

- **Science of Materials:** Organic materials that release light in response to electrical stimulation are used to construct OLED displays. To create the OLED, these organic materials—which are usually based on hydrogen and carbon structures—are layered in thin layers. The emissive layer, which produces light, the conductive layer, which moves electrons and holes, and the substrate, which offers structural support, are the three primary parts of an OLED display. The display's lifetime, brightness, and color accuracy are all impacted by the materials used. The overall performance and endurance of OLED displays have improved due to the creation of more stable and efficient organic compounds as a result of advancements in material science.

- **Production Procedures:** The encapsulation, patterning, and deposition of organic layers are some of the crucial processes in the production of OLED displays. Vacuum thermal evaporation (VTE), in which organic materials are heated in a vacuum chamber and subsequently condensed onto the substrate, is one of the most widely used techniques for depositing the organic layers. A further technique is inkjet printing, which is appropriate for high-resolution displays since it enables the exact deposition of organic components in predetermined patterns. The display is enclosed once the organic layers are deposited to shield it from elements like oxygen and moisture that might deteriorate the organic ingredients. To assure the quality and uniformity of the displays throughout the entire process, cleanroom settings and exact control over temperature and pressure are necessary.

3.3 OLED Displays' Advantages: Fast Response Times, Wide Viewing Angles, and Perfect Blacks

OLED technology is used for high-end displays because of its many important advantages, which include its quick response times, broad viewing angles, and capacity to create flawless blacks.

- **Flawless Blacks:** The ability of OLED panels to provide flawless blacks is one of their most praised characteristics. OLED displays may be fully turned off to create total darkness without any light leaking from nearby pixels because each pixel is self-illuminating. This feature yields an infinite contrast ratio, which is very helpful in settings that call for bright highlights and deep shadows. In low light or while viewing highly contrasted content, perfect blacks improve the entire visual experience by adding realism and immersion to visuals.

- **Broad Viewing Perspectives:** Consistent image quality is another area where OLED displays shine over a broad spectrum of viewing angles. OLED displays maintain their color fidelity and contrast even at sharp viewing angles, in contrast to standard LCDs, whose color and brightness can change when viewed from the side. This broad viewing angle is very useful in settings like living rooms or conference rooms when several people are watching the screen from various angles. OLED displays' adaptability and usability are enhanced by their consistent image quality, which remains intact regardless of viewing angle.

- **Quick Reaction Times:** Quick response times are one of OLED technology's main advantages. The speed at which a pixel can shift from one state to another, as from black to white or from one color to another, is known as a display's response time. OLEDs respond far faster than LCDs, with response times in the microsecond range. OLED displays are perfect for situations where quick image transitions are essential, such as gaming, sports broadcasting, and other situations where motion blur and ghosting are minimized due to their short response time.

3.4 Burn-in, Efficiency, and Cost Issues with OLED Technology

OLED technology, for all its advantages, is not without its problems. Burn-in, efficiency, and cost are just a few of the obstacles that the technology must overcome if it is to be widely adopted and function well over time.

- **Installation:** Burn-in, a phenomena where static images viewed for extended periods of time can leave a persistent ghost image on the screen, is one of the most well-known problems with OLED technology. This happens as a result of the organic ingredients in OLED pixels deteriorating at varying rates based on usage. In a video game, for instance, the pixels displaying a static logo or HUD element could deteriorate more quickly than those displaying other content, leaving apparent traces of the image even after the content has changed. Although manufacturers have introduced a number of solutions, including screensavers and pixel shifting, to lessen the effects of burn-in, long-term use is still problematic, especially in professional and gaming situations where static images are frequently displayed.

- **Performance:** OLED screens can use less energy than conventional LCDs when displaying bright, full-screen images, but they are more energy-efficient while displaying darker content. In contrast to an LCD display, which uses a continuous backlight, an OLED display uses more power to display a brilliant image because each pixel emits its own light. In situations where power efficiency is critical, including in mobile devices and battery-powered equipment, this unpredictable power usage may be a drawback. Although there is still a barrier to general adoption, improvements in OLED materials and driver circuits are intended to increase efficiency.

- **Expense Factors:** The other major obstacle is the expense of creating OLED displays. OLED displays are more expensive to build than conventional LED and LCD displays because of the intricate manufacturing process and high material costs. Because of the increased cost of production, OLED displays are now more expensive than other options on the market. Even though OLED technology has become less expensive over time, entry-level and mid-range markets still find it to be prohibitively expensive. Although more cost reductions are anticipated due to economies of scale and ongoing production developments, OLED technology is still more expensive than alternatives at the moment.

OLED technology is a widely sought-after option for high-end displays because it provides a distinct set of benefits such as flawless blacks, broad viewing angles, and quick response times. However, in order to guarantee its wider adoption and long-term viability, issues including burn-in, efficiency, and cost considerations need to be resolved. These difficulties should be lessened as technology develops, increasing the dependability and accessibility of OLED displays for a larger range of uses.

CHAPTER 4

Evaluation and Comparison: OLED vs. Mini-LED

4.1 Performance Metrics: A Comparative Study of Color Gamut, Brightness, Contrast, and Viewing Angles

It's critical to assess the performance of Mini-LED and OLED technologies over a range of critical parameters, such as brightness, contrast, color gamut, and viewing angles. These elements are crucial in establishing a display's overall quality and applicability for different uses.

- **Brightness:** When it comes to brightness, mini-LED screens usually outperform OLED. This is because of their sophisticated backlighting system, which produces a higher peak brightness level thanks to millions of tiny LEDs called Mini-LEDs. This is especially useful for HDR content that needs a high brightness in brightly light areas. However, the maximum brightness of OLED displays, which use self-emissive pixels, is lower. Better contrast and flawless blacks are OLEDs' way of making up for this, which can help brilliant elements stand out more against dark backgrounds.

- **Contrast:** Because OLED technology can produce genuine blacks, it has an unmatched contrast ratio. There is no light leakage since OLED pixels may be turned off entirely, which creates an infinite contrast ratio. Despite having a high contrast ratio, mini-LED screens fall short of OLED in this regard because they may bloom. Blooming is a side effect of the backlight structure that happens when light from bright areas spills into nearby dark areas. Local dimming zone improvements in Mini-LED displays, on the other hand, are closing this disparity and providing noticeably better contrast than conventional LED-LCDs.

- **Color Range:** Wide color gamuts can be achieved by both Mini-LED and OLED displays, however OLEDs often have a little advantage because of their pixel-level light control. OLEDs are perfect for applications that require exact color reproduction, such professional video editing, because they can create rich and realistic colors across a broad spectrum. Additionally, mini-LED displays have good color gamut performance, particularly when paired with quantum dot technology, which improves color saturation and accuracy. Still, OLED's emissive technical advantage puts it somewhat better in terms of overall color fidelity.

- **Viewing Angles:** OLED screens have better viewing angles than Mini-LED displays. Because of the self-emissive nature of their pixels, OLEDs remain bright and color-consistent even at very high viewing angles. Because of this, OLED is the best option in environments where a number of people from various postures will be seeing the display. Even while mini-LED displays are far superior to conventional LED-LCDs, they can still have some color shift and brightness reduction when viewed out of center, but these effects are less pronounced than with previous generations of technology.

4.2 Evaluation of Image Quality: Subjective and Objective Measures of Picture Effectiveness

A crucial component of display technology, image quality affects both user happiness and the whole viewing experience. Mini-LED and OLED display image quality is evaluated using both objective measurements (made using standardized testing methods) and subjective evaluations (based on personal perception).

- **Personal Evaluations:** The viewer's experience, which includes aspects like perceived brightness, color vibrancy, black level performance, and overall clarity, is frequently the focus of subjective assessments of image quality. OLED screens are widely acclaimed for producing a more engaging viewing experience with their deep blacks, brilliant colors, and superior contrast. OLED visuals are sometimes characterized by viewers as being more "cinematic," with a depth of detail that Mini-LED displays find difficult to match. On the other hand, mini-LEDs are renowned for their vivid and strong images, which makes them ideal for bright spaces or material that benefits from high peak brightness, such HDR movies or sports. It may come down to personal preference which one prefers: OLED is preferred by those who value contrast and color accuracy, whereas Mini-LED is preferred by those who value brightness and vividness.

- **Metrics with an objective:** With the use of specialist equipment, objective evaluations of image quality are carried out by measuring many aspects of display performance, including peak brightness, black levels, color accuracy, and uniformity. Because OLED displays can entirely disable individual pixels, they often perform better at the dark level. On the other hand, with enhanced local dimming, mini-LED displays can approach OLED in contrast ratio and perhaps reach higher peak brightness levels. Both technologies perform remarkably well in terms of color accuracy, particularly when paired with calibration tools that adjust color output to industry standards. OLED displays frequently score better in uniformity tests, which gauge the consistency of color and brightness across the panel, because they don't have a backlight structure.

4.3 Energy Efficiency and the Environment: Evaluating Power Usage and Environmental friendliness

When evaluating display technologies, energy efficiency and environmental effects are becoming more and more crucial, especially as manufacturers and consumers look to lessen their carbon footprint.

- **Power Requirement:** Since every pixel in an OLED display produces its own light, these displays often use less electricity when displaying darker images. Compared to Mini-LEDs, which use a backlight that uses energy even when showing black or dark content, OLEDs can be more energy-efficient in situations with a lot of black or dark parts. However, because many pixels must be powered at once in bright environments or while displaying white, OLEDs may lose some of their efficiency. Although mini-LED displays are more efficient than typical LED-LCDs in darker environments, they still fall short of OLED in bright scenes due to their sophisticated local dimming capabilities. Mini-LED displays may minimize power usage by dimming or turning off certain backlight zones.

- **Environmentality:** The materials and manufacturing techniques used to create OLED and Mini-LED displays have distinct effects on the environment. For example, OLED displays use organic components, which are generally less hazardous to the environment than some LED-backlighting systems' heavy metal content. OLED panels do, however, also require protective encapsulation, which may include non-recyclable materials, due to their increased sensitivity to oxygen and moisture. Even though they are made of more conventional materials, mini-LED displays have a longer lifespan and are more durable, which means that they require fewer replacements over time and have a less environmental impact. Both systems have disposal and recycling issues, and research is still being done to reduce the environmental impact of these technologies.

4.4 Cost Analysis: Comparing Mini-LED and OLED TVs' Price-to-Performance Ratios

The acceptance and market penetration of display technologies are significantly influenced by cost. Comprehending the Mini-LED and OLED TVs' price-to-performance ratio is crucial for both producers and customers.

- **Purchase Price at First:** OLED displays often cost more than Mini-LED displays because of the intricacy of their production and the high price of organic materials. OLED technology's self-emissive characteristic raises production costs because it demands accuracy and quality control. Though more expensive than conventional LED-LCDs, mini-LED displays are typically less expensive than OLEDs. The quantity of LEDs utilized in the backlight array and the complexity of the local dimming control are the main factors influencing the cost of mini-LED technology.

- **Value Over Time:** When assessing long-term value, OLED screens' greater image quality—especially with regard to contrast and black levels—often makes up for their higher initial cost. OLED has a strong value proposition for those that demand picture quality above all else and are prepared to spend more for a high-end viewing experience. But burn-in and lifespan issues can distort perceptions of value, particularly in settings where static images are regularly shown. Mini-LED displays may have superior long-term durability due to their strong brightness and lower burn-in risk, especially when watching a variety of content in bright rooms.

- **Rate of Price to Performance:** The particular requirements and preferences of the user determine the price-to-performance ratio of OLED and Mini-LED displays. OLED displays are perfect for professionals and movie buffs who need the best possible image quality since they offer unparalleled contrast and color accuracy. In contrast, mini-LED displays provide a good compromise between cost and functionality, especially for those who value longevity and brightness. When choosing between the two technologies, users typically weigh the importance of color purity and contrast against brightness and cost effectiveness.

Each technology Mini-LED and OLED has advantages and disadvantages that are particular to them. While OLEDs offer better contrast, color accuracy, and viewing angles at a greater cost and with some longevity issues, mini-LEDs are brighter and a more cost-effective option for people looking for high-quality displays. The user's specific needs, whether they focus on cost, environmental effect, energy efficiency, or image quality, should inform their choice between these two technologies. The differences between the two technologies might become less noticeable as they develop further, giving customers even more choices for high-performance displays.

CHAPTER 5

APPLYING DISPLAYS OUTSIDE OF THE LIVING ROOM

The uses of display technology have grown significantly beyond conventional living room configurations as a result of its progress. This chapter examines the wide range of display applications that are used in consumer electronics, business settings, automobile systems, and developing technologies, among other areas. We are able to have a thorough grasp of the ways in which display technologies are influencing the future by looking at the particular needs and advancements in these fields.

5.1 Consumer Electronics: Televisions, Computers, and Handhelds

Display technology is essential to the user experience in the world of consumer devices, impacting everything from work to enjoyment. TVs, monitors, and portable devices now have far better quality and greater versatility because of developments in display technology.

- **TVs (televisions):** Sleek, high-definition flat panels have replaced bulky cathode-ray tubes (CRTs) in modern televisions, marking a dramatic change in technology. Whether they are powered by OLED, Mini-LED, or QLED technology, today's TVs provide excellent picture quality with rich colors, deep blacks, and high dynamic range (HDR) features. Delivering an immersive viewing experience requires these qualities, especially as content continues to move toward higher resolutions like 4K and 8K. The consumer's priorities frequently determine which display technology they prefer for their TV; OLEDs are preferred for their contrast and color accuracy, while Mini-LEDs provide a brighter image better suited for well-lit areas.

- **Monitors:** Developments in display technology have also helped monitors, whether used for work or leisure. To provide a fluid and accurate visual experience, high refresh rates, short response times, and broad color gamuts are necessary. OLED displays are especially well-liked in the creative professions because of their excellent contrast and color reproduction, which are essential for jobs like graphic design, photo editing, and video creation. High refresh rates and quick response times often attained through cutting-edge LED or OLED technology give gamers a competitive edge and improve the gaming experience.

- **Portable Devices:** To produce high-resolution images and videos, portable devices such as laptops, tablets, and smartphones heavily rely on display technology. For example, smartphones that use OLED and AMOLED screens now have more brilliant displays, deeper blacks, and better energy efficiency. These screens are especially useful for photography, gaming, and content consumption, where user experience is greatly impacted by display quality. High-quality laptop displays with wide viewing angles and accurate color reproduction are in high demand, particularly from creative professionals and content makers who need dependable visual tools on the go.

5.2 Expert Exhibitions: Television, Film, and Electronic Signage

Displays used in professional settings must adhere to strict specifications for color accuracy, dependability, and longevity. In these situations, output, content production, and audience engagement can all be directly impacted by the caliber of display technology.

- **Studios:** Display technology is essential for jobs like color grading, video editing, and visual effects in film and television production facilities. OLED panels are the better option in these settings because of their excellent color accuracy and contrast ratio. Realistic blacks and a broad color gamut representation are crucial for guaranteeing that the finished result satisfies the highest requirements for visual quality. Furthermore, high-definition, large-format displays are utilized in virtual production stages. Here, LED panels are utilized to provide lifelike backgrounds and surroundings, completely changing the way visual effects are incorporated into live-action cinematography.

- **Aired:** Displays are employed in a variety of broadcast settings, including control rooms and on-air studios. Reliability, minimal latency, and accurate color reproduction are critical since inconsistencies can degrade live broadcast quality. In order to monitor several video feeds concurrently and guarantee that broadcasts keep a consistent visual quality, control rooms frequently employ OLED and high-end LED monitors. Additionally, in live sports broadcasting, where fast-moving material demands crisp and fluid graphics, sophisticated screens with high refresh rates and quick response times are essential.

- **Electronic Signage:** Digital signage plays a crucial role in corporate, retail, and public venues as a communication tool. Digital signage display technology selection is influenced by various aspects, including ambient illumination, viewing distance, and content needs. OLED and LED displays are widely utilized because of their longevity, brightness, and vibrant color. High-brightness LED displays are recommended for outdoor signs in order to guarantee visibility in direct sunlight, whilst inside displays could give priority to viewing angles and color fidelity. Displays become an effective tool for interaction and communication when interactive features like gesture recognition and touchscreens are incorporated into digital signage.

5.3 Infotainment systems, instrument clusters, and head-up displays in automobiles

Advanced display technologies are being used by the car industry more and more to improve vehicle operation, safety, and driver pleasure. Vehicle displays have developed from simple instrument clusters to intricate systems that offer entertainment, navigation, and real-time information.

- **Groups of Instruments:** Analog dials have given way to entirely digital displays in modern instrument clusters, which frequently make use of LCD, OLED, or Mini-LED technologies. These digital clusters come with programmable interfaces that show a variety of data, such as advanced driver-assistance systems (ADAS), speed, fuel levels, and navigation. Because OLED technology can create deep blacks and strong contrasts, it is very advantageous when used in instrument clusters. This makes it easier for drivers to see important information at a glance, even in varied lighting situations.

- **Sound and Vision Systems:** The main hub for entertainment, navigation, and car controls is an infotainment system. Modern cars come equipped with touch-sensitive, high-resolution displays that make a variety of amenities easily accessible to both drivers and passengers. OLED and capacitive touchscreens are widely utilized because of their longevity, clarity, and responsiveness. The user experience is further improved by the incorporation of speech recognition and connectivity technologies, which enable smooth interaction with music, navigation apps, and smartphones. Infotainment systems are increasingly adopting larger, curved screens, which provide a more engaging and user-friendly interface.

- **HUDs, or head-up displays:** With the use of head-up displays, drivers can view vital information without taking their eyes off the road by projecting it onto the windshield or a separate screen. In order to show information like speed, navigation, and safety alerts in a fashion that seems to float in the driver's field of vision, HUDs frequently use LED or laser projection technology. By eliminating the need for drivers to take their eyes off the road to examine their infotainment system or instrument cluster, this technology improves safety. The next development in car displays is augmented reality (AR) head-up displays (HUDs), which provide even more situational awareness by superimposing navigation instructions and hazard warnings directly onto the road ahead.

5.4 New Uses for Wearable Technology, Virtual Reality, and Augmented Reality

The frontier of display innovation is represented by emerging technologies like wearables, augmented reality (AR), and virtual reality (VR), which are pushing the envelope in terms of form factor, functionality, and user experience.

- **Wearable Technology:** To transmit information in a small and energy-efficient form, wearable devices such as smartwatches, fitness trackers, and augmented reality glasses rely on cutting-edge display technology. These devices frequently use OLED and AMOLED screens because of their thinness, flexibility, and power economy. OLED displays are perfect for wearable technology because they can create vivid colors and deep blacks, which are crucial for readability under different lighting circumstances and long battery life. The potential for even higher efficiency and brightness in micro-LED technology is expected to propel wearable display capabilities forward.

- **Surround Reality (AR):** By superimposing digital data over the physical world, augmented reality technology improves how users perceive their surroundings. In order to guarantee that digital elements are distinctly visible under varied lighting circumstances, screens that are not only transparent but also possess high resolution and brightness are needed. AR displays are usually built into gadgets like smart glasses, which project pictures straight into the user's line of sight via waveguides, holographic lenses, or micro-LEDs. In order to make AR displays discreet and comfortable to use for extended periods of time, it is difficult to strike a compromise between image quality, transparency, and comfort.

- **Virtual Reality (VR):** High-resolution, low-latency displays with a broad field of vision are necessary for VR technology, which immerses users in a fully digital world. OLED screens are frequently seen in virtual reality headsets because of their quick response times and deep blacks, which lessen motion blur and increase immersion. Manufacturers are investigating technologies like micro-LEDs and foveated rendering, which dynamically modifies the resolution based on the user's gaze, in response to the growing need for better resolutions and refresh rates in VR displays. The objective is to produce virtual reality (VR) experiences with lifelike graphics and seamless interactivity that cannot be distinguished from the real world.

Display technologies have become ingrained in many facets of our life and are not limited to conventional computer and television monitors. Displays have a significant impact on how we interact with information and the environment around us, from consumer gadgets to professional applications, automobile systems, and upcoming technology. These technologies will surely create new opportunities and alter the limits of visual experiences in several sectors as they develop further.

CHAPTER 6

TECHNOLOGICAL FRONTIERS: PROGRESS AND PROSPECTS FOR THE FUTURE

The industry is seeing ground-breaking inventions that push the limits of visual quality, efficiency, and versatility as display technologies continue to advance. This chapter analyzes hybrid display concepts, dives into the most recent developments in Mini-LED and OLED technologies, and talks about how artificial intelligence (AI) and machine learning might revolutionize display performance. These technological boundaries open up possibilities for applications that were previously thought of as science fiction, in addition to improving present display capabilities.

6.1 Mini-LED Innovations: Advanced Local Dimming, Micro LED, and Improvements to Mini LED Chips

Even though Mini-LED technology is already

groundbreaking, improvements are always being made to push its performance even farther. The development of Micro LED technology, improvements in local dimming methods, and developments in the production of Mini LED chips are some of the major innovations.

- **Technology of Micro LEDs:** The next development in LED technology, known as Micro-LED, is typified by increasingly smaller LEDs with increased brightness, endurance, and energy efficiency. In contrast to Mini-LED, which uses LEDs as a backlight, Micro LEDs work like individual pixels and are comparable to OLED technology but devoid of organic components. This leads to displays that are more resilient and less prone to burn-in, with the ability to generate flawless blacks and infinite contrast ratios. Because micro LED displays are scalable, they can be used for a variety of purposes, ranging from giant video walls to tiny wearable gadgets. The complicated and expensive production process for Micro LEDs, however, makes mass adoption extremely difficult.

- **Intelligent Local Dimming:** A crucial component of Mini-LED displays is local dimming, which gives users more control over contrast and brightness by modifying the light in particular areas of the screen. More accurate local dimming algorithms have been made possible by recent developments in this field, bringing the total number of dimming zones to thousands or even tens of thousands. This improves the display's capacity to create deeper blacks and lessens the phenomenon known as blooming, in which light objects seep into the screen's darker regions. Because of the enhanced control granularity, Mini-LED displays can now compete more successfully with OLED in terms of contrast and color accuracy.

- **Modifications to the Mini LED Chip:** The goal of ongoing research and development in mini LED chip technology is to make LEDs brighter and more efficient while keeping their size smaller. Improvements in chip design, such the use of quantum dot technology, have improved Mini-LED displays' color performance and energy economy even more. These improvements make it possible for screens to be thinner and more effectively manage heat, which makes them more appropriate for usage in ultra-slim mobile devices, TVs, and monitors. Furthermore, the cost of producing Mini-LEDs is steadily declining due to improvements in manufacturing techniques, opening up this technology to a wider market.

6.2 OLED Evolution: Flexible Displays, Stacked OLED, and Next-Generation Materials

OLED technology, which is renowned for its excellent image quality, is still developing thanks to advancements in flexible displays, layered OLED designs, and next-generation materials. These developments are expected to improve OLED displays' functionality and performance even more.

- **Subsequent Generation Resources:** The components utilized in the organic layers of OLED displays have a significant impact on their performance. The goal of recent research has been to create novel organic molecules with increased color purity, longevity, and efficiency. For instance, the addition of phosphorescent materials has allowed approximately 100% of electrical energy to be turned into light, greatly increasing the efficiency of OLEDs. Furthermore, the investigation of novel blue-emitting materials holds promise for improving the longevity and color accuracy of OLED displays, a historical shortcoming in OLED technology. These materials are essential to bringing OLED performance to the next level, particularly in high-end displays where brightness and color accuracy are critical.

- **OLED Stacking Technology:** A novel technique known as stacked OLED, or tandem OLED, involves stacking several OLED emitters on top of one another to produce a single pixel. This construction prolongs the display's life and improves its brightness and efficiency. Manufacturers can achieve higher color accuracy and greater energy efficiency in their displays by stacking multiple layers of red, green, and blue emitters. Applications requiring high brightness and durability, such outdoor signage and car displays, benefit greatly from stacked OLED technology. Additionally, this technique can assist in reducing some of the conventional issues with OLEDs, like burn-in and blue sub-pixel deterioration.

- **Adaptable Screens:** The field of flexible OLED displays is one of the most promising areas of display technology. The thin, flexible substrates used in these displays enable them to be bent, rolled, or even folded without impairing their functionality. Because of its adaptability, new product design opportunities are presented, leading to the creation of rollable TVs, foldable smartphones, and other cutting-edge form factors. Making sure these displays stay strong and functional over time—especially when bent or folded repeatedly—is the difficult part. These issues are being addressed by developments in materials science, such as the creation of flexible electrodes and more resilient encapsulation methods, which are opening the door for the mainstream use of flexible OLED displays.

6.3 Technology Convergence: Hybrid Display Ideas and MicroLED-OLED Composites

A rising number of people are interested in combining several technologies to develop hybrid displays that combine the best features of each as display technologies continue to progress. Combining OLED with Micro LED technology is one of the most exciting research directions.

- **Concepts for Hybrid Displays:** The goal of hybrid displays is to overcome the shortcomings of individual technology by utilizing the advantages of several. For instance, a hybrid display might incorporate OLEDs' higher contrast and color accuracy with Mini-LEDs' great brightness and energy economy. With this method, displays can have deep blacks for immersive viewing experiences and high peak brightness for HDR content, giving users the best of both worlds. Because hybrid displays can use different technologies depending on what is being presented, they may also be more energy-efficient. In applications like professional monitors, high-end televisions, and automobile displays where both brightness and contrast are crucial this convergence is especially pertinent.

- **Combinations of MicroLED and OLED:** The convergence of OLED and Micro LED technologies marks a major advancement in the field of display innovation. Manufacturers are able to produce displays that combine the brightness and endurance of Micro LEDs with the unmatched contrast and flexibility of OLED panels by merging Micro LEDs with OLED panels. This combination is especially useful for large-format displays, where it can be difficult to maintain consistent color accuracy and brightness throughout the panel. Furthermore, some of the disadvantages of each technology, such as the high production costs of Micro LEDs and the possibility of burn-in in OLEDs, can be lessened by using the hybrid technique. As a result, a brand-new class of displays has emerged that pushes the limits of durability, energy economy, and image quality.

6.4 The Functions of AI and Machine Learning: Optimizing Display and Intelligent Image Processing

The development and improvement of display technologies is becoming more and more dependent on artificial intelligence (AI) and machine learning. These cutting-edge computational methods are being applied to optimize display settings, boost picture processing, and increase user experience in general.

- **Intelligent Image Processing:** AI-powered techniques for image processing are revolutionizing how displays manage content. Based on the information being shown, these algorithms may analyze and modify the quality of an image in real time, improving details, lowering noise, and maximizing color reproduction. AI, for instance, may upscale photos to higher resolutions or improve their quality at lower ones without introducing artifacts. AI is capable of dynamically adjusting brightness and contrast of HDR content to maintain detail in both the image's bright and dark sections. A more engaging watching experience with crisper visuals, more accurate colors, and higher overall picture quality is the outcome of this clever processing.

- **Optimization of Display:** In addition, display settings are optimized using AI and machine learning according to user preferences and ambient factors. For example, AI can optimize visibility and comfort by adjusting a display's brightness, contrast, and color balance based on the ambient lighting conditions. Furthermore, AI is able to pick the optimal settings for various kinds of content, including games, sports, and movies, based on user interactions and preferences. This degree of personalization improves the user experience by offering the highest quality images for every given situation. Furthermore, by consuming less power when maximum brightness is not required, AI-driven optimization can improve energy efficiency.

- **AI's Prospects for Displays in the Future:** AI in display technology has more promise than just what is being used now. More advanced AI and machine learning algorithms may make it possible to interact with displays in new ways, like gesture detection, voice control, and personalized content recommendations. AI may also be used in the creation of next-generation display technologies, assisting in the design of more effective materials, streamlining production procedures, and even anticipating and resolving possible problems before they arise. An important step toward more intelligent, adaptable, and user-centric display technologies that can recognize and respond to user needs is the incorporation of AI into displays.

A new era in display innovation is being ushered in by the developments in Mini-LED, OLED, and hybrid display technologies as well as the revolutionary possibilities of AI and machine intelligence. As these technologies develop further, they will not only improve the performance and quality of displays but also increase their use in a variety of sectors and use cases. Future display technology should deliver previously unheard-of performance and user experiences, while being more dynamic, adaptable, and intelligent.

CHAPTER 7

Consumer Behavior and Market Dynamics

For all parties involved in the worldwide display industry manufacturers, retailers, and investors it is essential to comprehend market dynamics and customer behavior. This chapter offers a thorough examination of the size, segmentation, major players, and consumer trends of the global display market. It also looks at pricing tactics and the competitive environment, providing insights into potential market expansion and new trends.

7.1 The Size, Segmentation, and Major Players of the Global Display Market

Over the past ten years, the global display industry has grown significantly due to the spread of digital content, rising consumer demand for high-quality visual experiences, and technological developments. This section looks at the market's present size, how it is segmented, and the key companies that influence the sector.

- **Size of Market:** The global display market is a multibillion dollar sector that makes money from a variety of items, such as digital signage, smartphones, tablets, TVs, and monitors. The market for displays was estimated to be worth over $150 billion in recent years by market research, and it is anticipated to increase steadily going forward due to rising customer demand for cutting-edge display technologies including OLED, Mini-LED, and MicroLED.

Market Dividends: There are three main segments in the display market: technology, application, and region.

- **Technology Breakdown:** Leading display technologies that serve distinct market niches are LCD, OLED, MicroLED, and Mini-LED. OLEDs are the preferred choice for high-end consumer devices because of their improved image quality, but LCDs continue to dominate because of their cost and extensive use. Emerging technologies like micro-LED and mini-LED are progressively taking market share, particularly in high-end goods.

- **Segmentation of Applications:** Consumer gadgets like TVs, monitors, and cellphones are examples of displays in use, as are professional displays used in digital signage, broadcasting, and medical imaging. Furthermore, wearable technology, augmented and virtual reality (AR/VR) systems, and automobile displays are expanding market niches.

- **District Division:** North America, Europe, Asia-Pacific, and the rest of the globe make up the geographical segments of the market. Due to high levels of manufacturing and consumption of consumer electronics in nations like China, South Korea, and Japan, Asia-Pacific currently controls the majority of the market. Important markets are also represented by North America and Europe, especially for high-end screens and cutting-edge technologies.

Notable Players: The global display market is dominated by a few major companies and is extremely competitive.

- Leading the way in OLED technology, Samsung Display is a significant provider of screens for televisions, cellphones, and other consumer goods.

- **LG Display:** A major participant in the TV and monitor markets, LG Display is renowned for its innovations in OLED and LCD technology.

- **BOE Technology Group:** Based in China, BOE is a major producer of LCD panels and has been making inroads into the OLED market.

- **AU Optronics (AUO) and Innolux Corporation:** These two well-known LCD manufacturers are making investments in the creation of cutting-edge display technologies, like Mini-LED.

- **Apple, Sony, and Panasonic**: As well-known manufacturers of consumer electronics, these businesses set market trends by incorporating cutting-edge display technologies into their goods and promoting them.

7.2 Consumer Preferences and Trends: Elements Affecting Decisions About Display Purchases

The display market is significantly shaped by consumer behavior, since a range of factors such as evolving lifestyle trends, price sensitivity, brand loyalty, and technology preferences affect consumers' decision to buy. The main preferences and trends influencing customer behavior in the display market are examined in this section.

- **Technology Preferences:** OLED and Mini-LED display technologies, which provide better image quality, are becoming more and more popular among consumers.

- **OLED:** Perfect blacks, wide viewing angles, and quick response times are some of the features that make OLED technology so popular with consumers looking for high-end visual experiences, especially for gaming and home entertainment.

- **Mini-LED:** Mini-LED displays are becoming more and more popular as an improvement over conventional LCD technology because of its increased brightness, contrast, and energy economy. Mini-LED displays are frequently chosen by customers that value these characteristics but aren't ready to make the investment in OLED.

- **Nascent Technology:** Consumer preferences are also being influenced by the increasing availability and knowledge of MicroLED and Quantum Dot displays; early adopters are shown interest in these cutting-edge technologies.

Price Sensitivity: Consumer decision-making is still heavily influenced by price.

- **Entry-Level and Mid-Range categories:** Customers in these categories frequently value affordability over cutting-edge technology, which boosts sales of LCD screens because they provide a decent trade-off between price and performance.

- **Premium Segment:** On the other hand, customers in this market are more prepared to shell out more cash for cutting-edge technologies like OLED and Mini-LED because they place a higher value on attributes like improved picture quality, a sleeker appearance, and a prestigious brand.

- **Cost-Conscious Buyers:** Some buyers are still very sensitive to pricing, and they frequently choose reconditioned or older models in order to get the best deal possible at the lowest possible cost.

Brand Loyalty: Brand loyalty is an important factor to consider when making display purchase selections.

- **Largest Names:** Firms such as Samsung, LG, and Sony have established robust brand identities predicated on excellence, novelty, and dependability. Positive brand experiences increase the likelihood that customers will stick with these companies and buy their goods, even if they are more expensive.

- **Emerging Brands:** By providing competitive products at lower rates, emerging brands—especially those from Asia—are challenging more established competitors in the market and winning over consumers.

Lifestyle and Usage Trends: Consumers' changing display-related behaviors are influencing their purchase decisions.

- **Home Entertainment:** The popularity of gaming and streaming services has raised the need for high-definition monitors and big-screen TVs with excellent color accuracy and little latency.

- **Remote Work and Education:** As more people turn to online learning and remote work, there is a growing need for laptops and monitors with excellent screens since these users want settings that are productive and comfortable enough to use for extended periods of time.

- **Health and Well-Being:** Customers are searching for displays with eye-friendly characteristics including flicker-free technology and reduced blue light output as a result of growing knowledge of eye strain and the negative health effects of blue light.

7.3 Competitive Environment and Pricing Strategies: Evaluation of Market Pricing and Competition

Market dynamics in the display business are mostly determined by pricing tactics and the competitive environment. This section looks at pricing structures in various market segments and how pricing strategies are affected by competition.

Pricing Methods:

- **High-End Pricing:** Expensive display devices are usually more expensive, especially those that use OLED, MicroLED, or sophisticated Mini-LED technology. The manufacturers use the premium image quality, innovative features, and prestige of their brands to defend these higher pricing. This tactic aims to attract customers that value performance and brand value more than price.

- **Pricing for Penetration:** In fiercely competitive market niches, like LCD screens, producers could use penetration pricing techniques. This entails lowering prices in order to increase market share, especially when launching new models or in emerging countries. Although this method may result in reduced profit margins, it may improve sales volume.

- **Price Based on Value:** Value-based pricing is a strategy used by some firms, in which prices are determined not only by production costs but also by the perceived value to the buyer. In the mid-range market, when buyers are looking for a balance between performance and price, this tactic is frequently employed. Features like intelligence, energy efficiency, and attractive design can affect how much something is thought to be worth and, in turn, how much it costs.

- **Adaptive Costing:** Some businesses employ dynamic pricing tactics in reaction to market demand, modifying prices in response to variables like inventory levels, rival pricing, and seasonal demand. In online retail platforms, where prices are subject to regular fluctuations, this strategy is prevalent.

Market Leaders:

- **Competitive Landscape:** Firms such as Samsung, LG, and Sony hold a dominant position in the premium market, owing to their robust brand recognition and vast R&D capacities. Their capacity for innovation and the introduction of state-of-the-art technologies enables them to hold onto their market share while maintaining higher prices.

- **Difficulties:** By providing competitive products at lower rates, emerging brands especially those from China are upending the dominance of established competitors in the market. Global markets are seeing growth for companies like TCL and Hisense, especially in the value- and mid-range product categories.

- **Specialized Players:** Apart from the mainstream competitors, there exist specialist players who concentrate on particular markets, such medical imaging, automobile displays, or professional displays. Rather than only competing on pricing, these businesses frequently compete on technical specs, customization possibilities, and industry-specific certifications.

7.4 Prospects for the Future Market: Expanding Markets and Growth Estimates

A number of variables, such as changes in consumer behavior, the growth of emerging economies, and technical breakthroughs, will influence the worldwide display market in the future. In this section, growth projections are analyzed and major trends that are expected to impact the market in the upcoming years are identified.

Projections of Growth:

- **Continuous Growth:** The growing need for high-quality displays across a range of applications, including consumer electronics, automotive, and professional displays, is likely to fuel the worldwide display market's continued steady rise. Analysts estimate that in the next five to seven years, the market will be valued at more than $200 billion.

- **Innovation in Technology:** The market will increase primarily due to advancements in display technologies, such as the ongoing development of OLED, Mini-LED, and MicroLED. It is anticipated that the premium and mid-range segments will adopt these technologies more frequently as they become more affordable and accessible.

- **Updated Applications:** There will be a greater need for specialized displays as new applications like wearable technology, augmented reality, and virtual reality grow. These applications necessitate displays with special qualities, like flexibility, low latency, and high pixel density, which spurs innovation and market expansion in these specialized markets.

Asia-Pacific:

- **Emerging Markets:** Due to its robust manufacturing foundation in nations like South Korea, Japan, and China as well as expanding consumer demand in developing economies like

India and Southeast Asia, the Asia-Pacific region will continue to be the largest and fastest-growing market for displays. It is anticipated that government programs to encourage technological innovation and local production would also aid in the expansion of the market in this area.

- **Africa and Latin America:** There is a lot of room for expansion in Latin America and Africa as their economies continue to grow. The demand for consumer electronics, particularly displays, is anticipated to increase in these regions due to factors such growing internet penetration, rising disposable incomes, and increasing urbanization. Manufacturers may use cost-effective items that are suited to these new consumers' needs as part of their market penetration plans.

- **The Middle East and Eastern Europe:** These areas offer more room for expansion, especially in the case of mid-range and luxury display goods. It is anticipated that the growing use of digital technology in industries including healthcare, education, and retail would increase demand for business and professional displays.

Environmental and Sustainable Initiatives:

- **Green Technologies:** Sustainable and energy-efficient screens are in greater demand as environmental concerns rise. In order to comply with regulations and meet consumer expectations, manufacturers are investing in environmentally friendly technology, such as recyclable materials and screens with low power usage. Purchase decisions and future product development are likely to be influenced by this trend.

- **Social Responsibility (Sustainability):** Businesses are concentrating on lowering their carbon footprint, enhancing the sustainability of their supply chains, and encouraging ethical recycling methods as part of their growing integration of CSR activities into their business plans. These initiatives appeal to customers who care about the environment in addition to improving company reputation.

The global display market is growing at a dynamic rate due to changing customer tastes, growing market prospects, and technical improvements. Stakeholders in this quickly changing industry can better navigate the competitive landscape and seize new opportunities by understanding pricing tactics, market dynamics, and future trends.

CHAPTER 8

ENVIRONMENTAL RESPONSIBILITY AND SUSTAINABILITY

Sustainability and environmental responsibility are becoming crucial issues as the worldwide display business grows. This chapter explores energy efficiency and consumption, end-of-life management, sustainable initiatives, and the environmental impact of display manufacturing. Stakeholders may lessen the ecological footprint of the sector and make informed decisions by being aware of these factors.

8.1 The Display Manufacturing Industry's Environmental Impact: Material Sourcing and Production Procedures

Display technology production entails a number of intricate procedures and the usage of different materials, all of which have an impact on the environment. This section looks at how the display industry's material sourcing and production practices affect the environment.

Procurement of Materials:

- **Surplus Materials:** A number of raw materials are used in the production of displays, including glass substrates, metals (such aluminum, gallium, and indium), and rare earth elements. Significant environmental effects from the extraction and processing of these resources may include energy consumption, habitat damage, and pollution of the land and water.

- **Minerals in Conflict:** Conflict minerals include a number of commodities utilized in display technology, including tin, tungsten, and tantalum. In conflict areas, the mining of these minerals may be linked to violations of human rights and environmental deterioration. Businesses must now more than ever ensure that their supply chains are transparent and that these commodities are sourced sustainably.

Methods of Production:

- **Amount of Energy Used:** A significant amount of

energy is needed in the manufacturing of displays, especially those employing sophisticated technologies like OLED and Mini-LED. Carbon emissions are a result of this energy use, especially if it comes from non-renewable sources.

- **Use of Chemicals:** Adhesives, photoresists, solvents, and other chemicals are used in the display production process. Improper management of the handling and disposal of these substances may result in pollution of the environment. There is a push to utilize fewer dangerous chemicals and replace them with safer options.

- **Generation of Waste:** Waste products from manufacturing processes include scraps, byproducts, and damaged panels. To reduce the negative effects on the environment and make sure that waste is recycled or disposed of responsibly, proper waste management techniques are crucial.

8.2 Energy Use and Efficiency: Evaluating Mini-LED and OLED TV Power Usage

When assessing how display technologies affect the

environment, energy consumption is a crucial consideration. This section evaluates OLED and Mini-LED TV power consumption and compares their effectiveness to alternative display technologies.

Lightweight LED Energy Usage:

- **Backlight Mechanism:** Mini-LED displays provide for more exact control over contrast and brightness since they use a large number of miniature LEDs as the backlight source. As a result, it uses less energy than conventional LCDs with bigger backlight components. Because mini-LED displays can independently dim different parts of the panel, they can attain higher peak brightness levels while using less electricity.

- **Productivity Benefits:** Mini-LED technology's targeted dimming capabilities help save energy by obviating the requirement for backlighting the entire screen. Lower power usage in both bright and gloomy settings is a result of this efficiency.

Self-Emissive Technology:

- **OLED Energy Consumption:** Organic materials

used in OLED displays release light when an electric current is applied. OLEDs do not require a separate backlight, in contrast to LCDs and Mini-LEDs, which reduces the power loss associated with backlighting. Because individual pixels are entirely turned off, OLED displays can achieve great levels of energy efficiency, especially while displaying darker content. This results in lower power usage.

- **Difficulties:** OLED screens may use more power when displaying bright graphics or full-screen white backgrounds, despite their advantages in energy economy. This is because of the way OLED technology works, where the brightness of each pixel affects the total amount of power used.

Evaluative Comparison: The total energy efficiency of OLED versus Mini-LED displays varies depending on display settings, usage patterns, and content type. Although both technologies are better than conventional LCD panels, how well they perform in terms of energy depends on the content and application.

8.3 End-of-Life Management: Difficulties with Recycling and Disposal

The intricacy of the materials used makes recycling and disposing of display devices extremely difficult. The end-of-life management challenges related to display technologies are covered in this part along with the solutions used.

Difficulties with Recycling:

- **Complexity of Materials:** Multiple layers of materials, including glass, polymers, metals, and semiconductors, makeup display panels. Because of their intricacy, recycling these materials is difficult since unique tools and procedures are needed to separate and treat them.

- **Dangerous Elements:** Hazardous materials are present in some display technologies, including as lead solder connections and mercury in some backlighting configurations. Appropriate recycling procedures are required to manage these hazardous materials securely and avoid contaminating the environment.

Processes for Disposal:

- **Problems with Landfills:** When display devices are disposed of improperly in landfills, dangerous materials may leak into the groundwater and soil. Because of the possibility of harmful leaching and the lengthy decomposition durations involved, landfills are not the best place to dispose of electronic trash.

- **Management of E-Waste:** To handle the disposal of electronic gadgets, many nations have put in place recycling programs and e-waste management laws. By collecting, recycling, and securely discarding display devices, these programs hope to lessen their negative effects on the environment and encourage appropriate disposal techniques.

Projects for Recycling:

- **Programs for Manufacturers:** A number of display manufacturers have implemented recycling and take-back initiatives to make the process of gathering and handling end-of-life displays easier. These initiatives, which seek to recover valuable materials and cut waste, frequently involve collaborations with accredited e-waste recycling facilities.

- **Awareness of Consumers:** Increasing consumer knowledge of appropriate display device disposal and recycling is essential to enhancing end-of-life management. Public awareness efforts and convenient recycling locations support the promotion of ethical consumer behavior.

8.4 Industry Efforts to Minimize Environmental Footprint: Sustainable Initiatives

Reducing its environmental impact and focusing on sustainability are priorities for the display sector. The industry's numerous campaigns and efforts to encourage environmental stewardship are highlighted in this section.

Green Design:

- **Eco-Friendly Manufacturing:** In order to lessen the impact of their products on the environment, manufacturers are implementing green design concepts. This entails employing recyclable or biodegradable components, reducing the amount of hazardous elements used in display design, and increasing energy efficiency.

- **Energy-Sustainable Production:** Aims are being made to optimize production methods, use renewable energy sources, and lower energy consumption throughout the supply chain in order to increase the energy efficiency of manufacturing operations.

Recycled Materials:

- **Sustainable Materials:** Recycled materials are increasingly being used in display manufacture. Manufacturers are looking for ways to minimize waste and lessen their reliance on virgin resources by incorporating recycled metals, glass, and plastics into their new display items.
- **Replacement Materials:** There is continuing research into substitute, safer materials for display components. For instance, some businesses are creating displays that substitute conventionally dangerous materials with non-toxic, eco-friendly materials.

Standards and Certifications:

- **Environmental Certifications:** To show their dedication to sustainability, several display makers pursue environmental certifications like Energy Star, EPEAT, and RoHS (Restriction of Hazardous Substances). These certifications guarantee that goods fulfill strict safety and environmental requirements.

- **Industry Standards:** Guidelines and best practices for sustainable manufacturing and supply chain management are provided by industry-wide efforts and standards, such as the Global e-Sustainability Initiative (GeSI) and the Electronic Industry Citizenship Coalition (EICC).

CSR (Corporate Social Responsibility):

- **CSR Initiatives:** Display firms are working on lowering their carbon impact, funding community projects, and encouraging moral labor practices as part of their growing CSR programs. CSR initiatives improve the company's image while having a good effect on the environment and society.

- **Partnerships and Collaborations:** The industry is working together to address sustainability issues and advance group efforts towards a greener future through partnerships and collaborations with environmental organizations, governmental bodies, and other stakeholders.

The display business must take sustainability and environmental responsibility seriously. The industry may lessen its ecological footprint and contribute to a more sustainable future by managing end-of-life disposal, addressing the environmental impact of production processes, increasing energy efficiency, and putting sustainable initiatives into place.

CHAPTER 9

A Buyer's Guide to OLED and Mini-LED TVs

It's important to comprehend a variety of technological factors and how they affect performance when thinking about a new TV, especially with regards to cutting-edge technologies like OLED and Mini-LED. Through an exploration of major features and specs, display size and resolution, HDR performance, and other significant variables, this chapter offers a thorough guidance to assist customers in making informed judgments.

9.1 Important Characteristics and Details: Recognizing Technical Terms

It is essential to comprehend the technical jargon related to both technologies in order to make an informed decision when choosing between Mini-LED and OLED TVs. The important characteristics and requirements are explained in this section.

Resolution:

- **4K vs. 8K:** Resolution is what controls how clear a picture appears on the screen. Four times as much detail is available in 4K (Ultra HD) as in Full HD (1920 x 1080 pixels), thanks to its resolution of 3840 x 2160 pixels. Even more information is available with 8K resolution (7680 x 4320 pixels), although there is still a dearth of 8K broadcasts and material.

- **Density of Pixels:** More pixels on the screen equals higher resolution, which helps create crisper, more detailed images. Picking a TV that offers the appropriate level of information based on screen size is made easier by having a solid understanding of pixel density.

Hertz (Hz):

- **Refresh Rate:** The number of times per second that the image on the screen is updated is known as the refresh rate, and it is expressed in Hertz (Hz). Smoother motion is achieved with higher refresh rates (e.g., 120Hz or 240Hz), which is advantageous for fast-moving material, video games, and sports viewing.

- **Motive Management:** Higher refresh rate TVs typically handle motion better, minimizing motion blur and enhancing the overall viewing experience.

Difference Ratio:

- **Static versus Dynamic:** The contrast ratio calculates the difference between the TV's blackest and whitest possible images. Brighter whites and deeper blacks are indicative of a higher contrast ratio. OLED displays can totally turn off individual pixels, which allows them to generally offer greater contrast ratios.

- **Local Dimming:** By independently dimming particular regions of the screen, mini-LED TVs can increase contrast and overall image quality.

Color Gamut:

- **Color Accuracy**: The range of colors that a TV can display is referred to as color gamut. More accurate and vivid colors are a result of technologies like HDR (High Dynamic Range) and wide color gamut standards (like DCI-P3).

- **Color Depth:** The amount of colors a TV can display is determined by color depth, which is expressed in bits. Images with greater detail and more seamless color transitions are produced by higher color depth.

9.2 Screen Dimensions and Resolution: Complying with the Viewing Environment

For the best viewing experience, select the appropriate display size and resolution. Advice on choosing screen size depending on your viewing environment is given in this section.

Screen Size:

- **Distance to View:** The distance at which you plan to watch determines the optimal screen size. As a general rule of thumb, the viewing distance for a 4K TV should be between 1.5 and 2.5 times the screen size. A 65-inch TV, for instance, may be viewed from 8 to 13 feet away.

- **Room Dimensions and Design:** Take into account the size of your space and where you want the TV to be. Smaller displays might work better in cramped places, while larger screens might be more suitable for rooms with more open areas.

Thoughts Regarding Resolution:

- **4K Resolution:** In most cases, 4K resolution provides enough clarity and detail for most viewing angles and screen sizes. Large screens work well with it, and it offers a discernible upgrade above Full HD.

- **High Definition:** Even while 8K provides incredibly fine resolution, its advantages are more noticeable at tight viewing angles or on very big screens. Since there is currently a dearth of 8K content, 8K TVs are a more specialized option.

Angle of Viewing:

- **Direct versus Off-Angle Viewing:** Think about how frequently viewers will view the TV from various perspectives. OLED TVs often provide a larger spectrum of consistent color and brightness, as well as improved viewing angles. Viewing Mini-LED TVs from off-angles may cause minor color and brightness fluctuations.

9.3 High Dynamic Range Performance: Evaluating Capabilities

High Dynamic Range (HDR) increases color accuracy, brightness, and contrast to improve visual quality. How to evaluate Mini-LED and OLED TVs' HDR performance is covered in this section.

HDR10:

- **HDR Formats:** HDR10, the most popular HDR format, offers more contrast and brightness than standard dynamic range (SDR). It is a common feature in many TVs and is extensively supported.
- **Dolby Vision:** Dynamic metadata, a feature of Dolby Vision, optimizes picture quality by modifying HDR settings scene-by-scene or frame-by-frame. Generally speaking, it performs better than HDR10.
- **HDR10+:** Like Dolby Vision, HDR10+ improves HDR performance with dynamic metadata. Certain TVs and streaming services support it.

Highest Brightness:

- **Levels of Brightness:** One major factor affecting HDR performance is a TV's maximum brightness setting. Improved HDR effects and more vibrant highlights are made possible by higher peak brightness levels. In comparison to OLEDs, mini-LED TVs usually have higher peak brightnesses, which can improve HDR performance in bright spaces.

Black Levels and Contrast:

- **OLED vs. Mini-LED:** Because of their self-emissive technology, which produces true blacks and excellent contrast ratios, OLED displays excel in contrast and black levels. While local dimming is used by mini-LED TVs to enhance contrast, they might not attain the same level of blackness as OLED TVs.

9.4 Things to Think About: Spending Limit, Lighting in the Room, and Content Consumption Patterns

A number of pragmatic considerations need to be made when buying a TV in order to make the optimal selection for your requirements and surroundings. Important factors including budget, lighting in the space, and content consumption patterns are covered in this section.

Amount Allotted:

- **Comparison of Costs:** OLED and mini-LED TVs are available at various pricing points. OLEDs are often more costly because of their cutting-edge technology and excellent image quality. Small-LEDs are a more cost-effective substitute for conventional LCDs that also perform better.

- **Purchase Value:** Think about the benefits of performance and features in relation to price. Depending on your preferred viewing experience, decide if the extra cost for features like HDR performance or better resolution is justified.

Environment Lighting:

- **Ambient Light Conditions:** Various display technologies may operate differently depending on the lighting in your environment. OLED TVs have excellent contrast and black levels, making them ideal for spaces that are dark or partially illuminated. Since ambient light can degrade picture quality in bright settings, mini-LED TVs perform better due to their higher peak brightness.

- **Light Control:** Take into account having some control over the lighting in your viewing space. While rooms with different lighting circumstances may benefit from Mini-LEDs brightness and versatility, OLED's deeper blacks can be advantageous in regulated lighting environments.

Habits of Content Consumption:

- **Category of Content:** Examine the kinds of information you watch most often. Prioritize characteristics like high resolution, refresh rate, and HDR performance if you enjoy watching sports, movies, and playing video games in high definition. Good color accuracy and a normal 4K resolution might be enough for everyday TV watching or streaming.

- **Processes of Use:** Take into consideration the TV's intended usage and frequency of use. Regular gamers or movie buffs might choose an OLED or premium Mini-LED for its improved performance, but casual viewers could find a less expensive alternative.

Thorough examination of important features, display size, resolution, HDR performance, and practical considerations like budget and room conditions are necessary when deciding between Mini-LED and OLED TVs. Customers can choose a TV that best suits their needs and tastes by being aware of these factors and making educated judgments.

CHAPTER 10

BEYOND OLED AND MINI-LED: THE FUTURE OF DISPLAY
TECHNOLOGY

The field of display technology is always changing, with new developments on the horizon that could completely transform visual perception. This chapter investigates display technology's future, looking at new and developing technologies, possible innovations, the larger display ecosystem, and the changing visual experience.

10.1 New Developments in Display Technologies: Quantum Dot, Laser TV, MicroLED, and Projection

A number of new technologies are emerging as display technologies progress, each with special advantages and possible uses.

Small LED:

- **Overview of Technology:** Tiny, individual LEDs are

used in microLED technology to form pixels. Since each MicroLED generates light independently, there is no need for a backlight and exact control over color and brightness is possible. Wide color gamuts, deep blacks, and excellent contrast ratios are the promises of this technology.

- **Perks:** Excellent brightness levels, high contrast ratios, and energy efficiency are features of microLED displays. In addition, they last longer and offer better color fidelity than conventional LED and OLED technology.

- **Difficulties:** The main obstacles are complicated and expensive production processes, as well as problems with expanding the technology to accommodate big displays.

Quantum Dot:

- **Overview of Technology:** Quantum dots, which are tiny semiconductor particles, are used in quantum dot displays. When exposed to light, they release particular colors. These dots are frequently combined with LED backlighting to improve brightness and color accuracy.

- **Perks:** When compared to conventional LCDs, Quantum Dot technology offers better color accuracy, brightness, and energy economy. It offers improved HDR performance and a broader color range.

- **Difficulties:** Costly as they may be, quantum dot displays are still a developing technology with constant research being done to enhance their effectiveness and performance.

Laser TV:

- **Technology Overview:** Laser TVs project images onto a screen by using lasers as a light source. Wide viewing angles, brilliant colors, and great brightness levels are all possible with this technology.

- **Perks:** Laser TVs are ideal for large-screen applications because of their superior brightness and color accuracy. In addition, they have a longer lifespan than the conventional projector bulbs.

- **Difficulties:** Laser projectors and screens can be expensive, and the size and area needed for installation may provide difficulties.

Technology Overview:

- **Projection Displays:** Projectors are used in projection displays to project images onto a surface or screen. High-resolution projectors that produce huge, high-quality images and ultra-short throw projectors are examples of innovations in this field.

- **Perks:** huge screen sizes and immersive experiences are possible with projection displays, which are frequently less expensive than huge flat-panel displays. They can be utilized in a variety of contexts and are also adaptable.

- **Difficulties:** Projectors can have problems with color accuracy and maintenance requirements, and they may need controlled lighting settings for best results.

10.2 Technological Advancements: Possible Disruptive Ideas and Their Significance

Potential innovations that have the potential to have a big impact on the market will also shape display technology in the future.

Flexible and Foldable Displays:

- **Overview:** Materials that permit screens to bend and fold without causing damage are used in flexible displays. There are currently some smartphones and tablets using this technology, and it may find use in other consumer gadgets as well.

- **Result:** Rollable TVs, folding smartphones, and wearable displays are just a few of the novel form factors and uses that flexible displays can make possible. They provide increased adaptability and creative design in their devices.

8K and Beyond:

- **Overview:** With four times as many pixels is 4K, 8K resolution offers a noticeable improvement in detail. Researchers are investigating resolutions even higher than 8K.

- **Result:** Improved visual clarity and detail are promised by 8K displays, particularly for large screens. Because they offer more vivid and immersive pictures, they have the potential to change industries like virtual reality and professional film production.

Virtual Reality (VR) and Augmented Reality (AR) Displays:

- **Overview**: As AR and VR technologies evolve, so do its display options, which now provide greater comfort, better field of vision, and higher resolutions.

- **Result:** The way we engage with digital material is changing as a result of AR and VR displays, which offer immersive experiences for training, gaming, and simulation. The usefulness and realism of these applications will increase with advancements in display technology.

10.3 The Display Ecosystem: Including Other Services and Technologies

The development of display technologies will not only revolve around improving panels; it will also involve integrating these technologies with other services and systems.

Smart Home Technology Integration:

- **Overview:** With features like voice control, home automation integration, and smart assistants, displays are becoming a crucial part of smart home ecosystems.

- **Result:** More smooth interactions with displays are made possible by integration with smart home systems, which also makes it possible to use features like voice-activated control, automation according to user preferences, and networking with other smart devices.

Streaming and Cloud Computing Services:

- **Overview:** Display technology is being impacted by the way content is distributed and consumed, which is being changed by cloud computing and streaming services.

- **Result:** Advanced HDR formats, high-bandwidth streaming, and interactive content will all need to be supported by displays. The way that material is viewed and enjoyed across various devices will continue to evolve thanks to cloud-based services.

Artificial Intelligence (AI) and Machine Learning:

- **Overview:** By using intelligent picture processing, upscaling, and personalized content recommendations, AI and machine learning are being used to improve display performance.

- **Result:** AI-driven improvements can offer personalized experiences, adjust display settings according to viewing conditions, and increase picture quality. The user experience and display technologies will advance as a result of this integration.

10.4 Final Thoughts: The Changing Visual Experience

Exciting developments in display technology are anticipated to completely change the way we interact with visual content in the future. The display landscape is changing quickly, thanks to innovations in flexible displays, integration with smart systems, and new technologies like Quantum Dot and MicroLED.

- **Welcome to Innovation:** New technologies will

come with more uses, more flexibility, and better performance. Keeping up with these developments is essential for taking advantage of the newest inventions and making wise selections.

- **Resultant Effect on Customer Experience:** The way that customers interact with and enjoy visual material will continue to be impacted by the continual progress of display technology. The future of visual experiences will be shaped by advancements in form factors, display quality, and technology integration.

In conclusion, there is a lot of promise and room for expansion in the field of display technology in the future. Consumers, producers, and tech enthusiasts may better navigate the changing landscape and embrace the next generation of visual experiences by knowing these developing trends and developments.

ABOUT THE AUTHOR

 Author and thought leader in the IT field Taylor Royce is well known. He has a two-decade career and is an expert at tech trend analysis and forecasting, which enables a wide audience to understand complicated concepts.

Royce's considerable involvement in the IT industry stemmed from his passion with technology, which he developed during his computer science studies. He has extensive knowledge of the industry because of his experience in both software development and strategic consulting.

Known for his research and lucidity, he has written multiple best-selling books and contributed to esteemed tech periodicals. Translations of Royce's books throughout the world demonstrate his impact.

Royce is a well-known authority on emerging technologies and their effects on society, frequently requested as a speaker at international conferences and as a guest on tech podcasts. He promotes the development of ethical technology, emphasizing problems like data privacy and the digital divide.

In addition, with a focus on sustainable industry growth, Royce mentors upcoming tech experts and supports IT education projects. Taylor Royce is well known for his ability to combine analytical thinking with technical know-how. He sees a time when technology will ethically benefit humanity.

www.ingramcontent.com/pod-product-compliance
Lightning Source LLC
LaVergne TN
LVHW051701050326
832903LV00032B/3945